1995

J
590
SUS
Sussman, Susan
LIES (PEOPLE BELIEVE) ABOUT
ANIMALS

LIES (People Believe) ABOUT ANIMALS

By Susan Sussman and Robert James

Photographs by Fred Leavitt

Albert Whitman & Company, Morton Grove, Illinois

We wish to thank the many people whose generosity of time, knowledge, facilities, and support contributed to the spirit, research, direction, and completion of this book: Carol McKechnie; Dr. Robert Keough and Madlynn Di Iacova-Tomei of the Cook County, Illinois, Department of Animal Control; Thomas Stice, alligator researcher for the Florida Game and Fish Commission; The Chicago Herpetological Society; Lani Witt; Cathy and Ted Paul; Karen and Bob Totten; Monte Musgrove, D.V.M.; Lorna Sifford, D.V.M.; Dr. Bhagavan Antle of the Buckingham Zoological Park, Buckingham, Virginia; Lincoln Park Zoo, Chicago, Illinois; Hansen's Disease Center, Carville, Louisiana; Jane Jordan Browne, literary agent; Margit Leavitt; and our editor, Kathleen Tucker.

Designed by Margit Wevang Leavitt

Library of Congress Cataloging-in-Publication Data

Sussman, Susan.
  Lies (people believe) about animals.

  Summary: Presents commonly held beliefs about bats, tarantulas, snakes, porcupines, and other animals and then explains the surprising truths.
    1. Animals—Miscellanea—Juvenile literature.
[1. Animals—Miscellanea] I. James, Robert, 1944-
II. Leavitt, Fred, 1941- ill. III. Title.
QL49.S845 1987   590   86-15949
ISBN 0-8075-4530-9

For Donna Chocol, who insisted I go
see the man with the baby ostrich
— *S.S.*

For Marilyn Price
— *R.J.*

For Adam
— *F.L.*

CONTENTS

ALLIGATORS

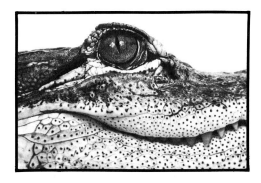

LIE: Alligators often attack people.

TRUTH: Alligators rarely attack people.

Alligators know the difference between their natural prey and humans. In Florida, home to nearly a million alligators, records show just five definite and two suspected alligator-caused deaths over the last *thirty years*. If you swim in Florida's fresh waters, there is a ninety-five percent probability an alligator is nearby. Obviously, if a million alligators liked the taste of people, there would be many more deaths. "Accidents," the word alligator experts use to describe biting incidents, average five a year. They are called accidents because these bites are provoked attacks caused by people trying to tease or catch alligators or people who feed alligators and hold onto the food too long. Although alligators don't normally attack humans, they *will* defend themselves—either by biting or by lashing out with their mighty tails—when they feel threatened.

When an alligator dives under water, it becomes as airtight as a submarine. Strong muscles clamp its nose shut. Special flaps of skin keep water out of its throat and ears. Thin second eyelids, clear enough for the alligator to see through, cover its eyes. An alligator can stay submerged twenty minutes in warm water and an hour or more in cold water, which slows its body functions.

Alligators, North America's largest reptiles, are sluggish critters who spend their days floating and sunning. Because they have poor salivary glands and cannot produce spit, alligators prefer to hunt and eat in the water, using it to help them swallow. Alligators are the garbage trucks of the waterways. They eat fish, shrimp, turtles, crayfish, frogs—and even birds, small mammals, and dead animals.

ARMADILLOS

LIE: The armadillo is a reptile.

TRUTH: The armadillo is a mammal.

The armadillo's bumpy coat of armor certainly makes it *look* like a relative of the turtle or alligator. But the armadillo, like all mammals, is warm-blooded, has hair, and gives birth to live young, instead of hatching eggs.

Armadillos are usually named for the number of flexible, overlapping bands down their backs, as few as three or as many as twenty-two. The species found in the United States is the nine-banded armadillo, which migrated here from Mexico in the mid-1800s and now numbers in the millions.

One reason our armadillo population has grown so fast is they are always born four at a time (in two sets of identical twins, all male or all female). Also, their thick armor holds off enemies while the armadillo quickly digs a burrow. One favorite survival trick is to jump straight up in the air, startling an enemy long enough for the armadillo to escape to safety. Unfortunately, many an armadillo resting on the warm asphalt of a highway has died trying to jump up and scare away a rapidly approaching car. Although cartoons show armadillos rolling into tight balls to protect their soft underbellies, only the three-banded and pigmy armadillos can do this.

Armadillos can carry leprosy, or Hansen's disease, a horrible illness that has killed or disfigured humans for centuries. Through recent armadillo/leprosy research begun in Louisiana by Dr. Eleanor Storrs and Dr. Waldemar Kirchheimer, armadillos are now helping win the war against leprosy. Armadillo colonies are being maintained in various parts of the world for the purpose of producing leprosy germs to be used for vaccination studies.

Three-banded armadillo

BATS

LIE: Bats are blind. This is where we get the expression "blind as a bat."

TRUTH: Bats aren't blind. Bats can see about as well as people.

It was once thought bats were blind because of the jumpy way some of them swoop up, down, and around in the night sky. We now know bats can see in daylight but not at night. The problem is that bats are *nocturnal*, resting during the day and feeding at night. Finding food in the dark can be tricky. Luckily, bats have a special way of using their mouths and ears to "see" in the dark.

With mouths open wide, bats shout a special sound as they fly, a sound too high for us humans to hear. (The bat sounds we *can* hear are not food-finding cries, but the much lower-pitched squawks of bats complaining or calling to one another.) When the sound hits something—a moth, a tree, a firefly—it bounces an echo back to the bat. This is called *echolocation.* The bat can tell one echo from another, which is why it will gobble up the moth and firefly but not the tree. If a bat swoops towards you, as bats will do, it's because its sound waves are bouncing off your buttons, barrettes, etc. As soon as the bat realizes those small objects are not bugs, it will swerve away.

All bats can get around by echolocation, but it is particularly important to the insect eaters, which must catch flying insects at night. These bats catch up to one and a half times their body weight every night. (Can you imagine, if you weigh fifty pounds, trying to eat seventy-five pounds of food in one day? Burp!) If you blindfold a bat and put it in a dark room, it will still find its way around. But if you cover its eyes *and* ears, it will bump into things.

Different species of bats eat different foods: insects, fruit, nectar, fish, birds, and rodents. One of the strangest

Big brown bat

diets belongs to the vampire bat, whose favorite food is blood. Unlike Count Dracula, who "vants to suck your blood," real vampire bats avoid humans. These South American and African bats prefer dining on the blood of wild animals, horses, cows, and barnyard fowl such as chickens.

To eat, the vampire bat bites an animal with its razor-sharp front teeth. The teeth are so sharp that the bite is rarely painful enough to wake the sleeping animal. As blood from the bite seeps out, the bat laps it up the way a cat laps milk. It takes about twenty minutes for the bat to drink its fill. When it's done, the cut closes, and the animal stops bleeding. The bat takes such a small amount of blood that the animal is not hurt. Like most bats, the vampire is timid. It avoids other nocturnal animals and feeds only on *diurnal* animals (animals that sleep at night). The biggest problem with vampire bats is that their bites can carry disease from one animal to another. Some people believe vampire bats live only on blood, but if they're hungry enough they'll also eat bugs and mice.

Centuries ago, bats were believed to be a kind of bird and were sometimes called "witches' birds." But bats are flying mammals and very different from birds. Bats do not lay eggs as birds do. Instead, baby bats are born alive, just like people, dogs, cats, and all other mammals. Mother bats nurse their young with their own milk. And bats are covered with soft fur instead of feathers.

Bats are neat, cleaning their bodies and wings often. They don't have fleas because they eat them! They must keep their wings—those long, slender fingers covered with skin—in perfect condition. Some bats have more wing to clean than others. Giant fruit bats, the largest in the world, may have wings that measure five feet from one tip to the other. By contrast, bamboo bats are as small as your thumb.

A good bat-watching place is Carlsbad Caverns in New Mexico. Each evening at sundown, millions of bats fly out of the caverns for a night of insect eating. A special amphitheater has been built so people can sit and watch this awesome event. The bats begin returning around midnight and by dawn are all safely inside. They groom themselves and sleep until nightfall, when it is time to hunt for food again.

Bats occasionally fly into a home through an open window or down a chimney. If a bat must be removed from your home, the person doing it should protect his or her hands with gloves, turn on a light to keep the bat still, and then gently gather the bat and place it outside. It is also possible to call your local animal control department and ask for help.

It is wise never to try to capture a bat unless you must usher it out of your house. There are two good reasons for this. First, bats are *carnivores* (meat eaters), and all carnivores can carry a disease called *rabies*, which is dangerous to people. If you see a bat that can't fly or appears dizzy or hurt, it might have rabies, and you must stay clear. (It might also have the flu or a stomachache, but you shouldn't take a chance.)

Second, if you capture a healthy bat and put it in a cage, the poor bat will almost surely die. A bat eats so many different kinds of bugs that it is nearly impossible for a nonscientist to feed it a healthy, balanced diet. Besides, we need all the bug eaters we can get to help control mosquitoes, flies, and other outdoor pests.

BEARS

LIE: Bears hibernate all winter.

TRUTH: Some bears sleep more in winter, but none are true hibernators.

True hibernators (like the groundhog) enter a deathlike sleep in which their body temperatures drop, they barely breathe, and their hearts hardly beat. Body functions of most bears slow only slightly in winter. They still get up occasionally and move around, leaving their dens to forage for food. And some bears, like the male polar bear, grizzly bear, and bears in warm climates, may not enter a winter sleep at all.

Unlike the Papa Bear in "Goldilocks," a real papa bear does not stay with his family. Soon after the male mates with the female, he wanders off. The female bear gives birth in her den around January or February. The inch-and-a-half-long babies are born blind and bald. One of the fastest-growing animal babies in the world, baby bears will weigh ten to fifteen pounds by the time they leave the den in spring. The female must protect her cubs from males, who have been known to eat baby bears.

Bears can't see very far, but they make up for it with keen senses of smell and hearing. They are *omnivores*, eating all sorts of animals and vegetables. With their long claws, they scoop salmon from a stream or dig juicy roots from the ground.

One of the mysteries of bears is "bear trees." Bears stand on their hind legs, stretch as tall as they can, and then grab and claw and bite these trees. Since this is most often done by male bears, it is believed bears are leaving their mark and scent on trees to warn away bears from other territories. For some reason one tree in an area will be used as a bear tree while the others are left untouched.

Himalayan black bear

ELEPHANTS

LIE: Elephants drink through their trunks.

TRUTH: Elephants drink through their mouths, like all animals.

Elephants *seem* to drink through their trunks but are really using them like giant straws to suck up gallons of water. They either squirt the water into their mouths for a drink or spray it over their bodies. The amazing trunk is a six-foot-long nose that the elephant uses for much more than breathing and smelling. It is controlled by forty thousand muscles, and the elephant uses it to pick up the tiniest peanut from the ground or haul huge timbers in the teak forests of Thailand. It can be used as a hand to strip leaves and bark from trees and to pick brush and grass from fields and feed them into the elephant's mouth. The trunk is delicate enough to pat a baby elephant and powerful enough to smash a lion.

Elephants are the largest living land mammals in the world. Like all of the large land mammals, they are *herbivores*, or plant-eating animals. They sleep only four to six hours a day since most of their lives must be spent looking for and eating food. It takes a lot of leaves and grass to fill up animals weighing ten to twelve thousand pounds! Each day, an adult elephant eats four to six hundred pounds of vegetation and drinks sixty gallons of water.

There are two kinds of elephants, Asian and African. The Asian elephant's ears are small, and it has a bump on the top of its head. The African elephant is bigger than the Asian and has large, floppy ears and a forehead that slants into the trunk like a slide. Asians are often used as circus elephants because they have a gentler nature than Africans and are easier to train.

African elephant

In India there is an elephant school where young elephants are trained for four years to work in the teak forests. The lucky young men who are chosen to be *mahouts* (elephant men) are each given an elephant to train and care for. Man and elephant form a team that will last until one of them dies.

Some people say elephants never forget. Elephants do seem to remember where the good food is, who is nice to them, and, more importantly, who isn't nice to them. But mahouts know elephants forget like any other animal, and it is only after careful training that elephants remember tasks they are taught.

Female elephants, called cows, carry their babies for nearly two years before giving birth, longer than any other mammal. Some time after twenty to twenty-three months of pregnancy, the two-hundred-pound baby is born. It is covered with dark black hair that will disappear as it grows older. When a cow is giving birth, another cow, called the auntie, comes to help. After the baby is born, the auntie cares for it until the mother is able. The male elephants, called bulls, do not stay with the herd of cows and young elephants. They are loners, standing apart from the others and watching out for danger.

Elephants seem to share many of our emotions. Members of a herd, mostly cows and babies, are like a family. They often stroke each other or touch their trunks in greeting, and mothers pat and hug their babies. Elephants display both joy and sadness. When elephants are happy, a sweet-smelling fluid drips from glands on either side of their heads. When they are sad, perhaps because a member of the herd has died, some will cry.

Although elephants have very thick skin, they can't stand heat and must be careful not to get sunstroke. To moisten and cool their skin, they suck water up their trunks and then spray it out over their bodies. Sometimes they roll around in the mud to cool their skin and prevent insect bites. When many elephants roll around in the same place, they create mud pits deep enough to catch water and form small watering holes. Mud-covered elephants are always messy and sometimes look weird. In Africa's Tsavo Park, for example, elephants turn red from rolling in the red clay along the riverbank.

The tusks on either side of an elephant's trunk are long, curved *incisors* (teeth) made of a material called ivory. An elephant's baby tusks fall out when the elephant is about two years old. New tusks grow in and will grow slowly as long as the elephant lives. An adult's tusks are around eight to ten feet long and are used to dig, lift, and fight. For many years people killed elephants for their tusks, which were then mounted as decorations or made into items like jewelry, statues, and piano keys. Today, most elephants live on government reserves where there are laws protecting them from hunters. And, luckily for elephants, piano keys are now made of plastic!

Elephants don't have particularly good eyesight, and they can't turn their heads very easily. They are warned of danger by their keen sense of smell and by their sharp hearing. If the wind is blowing at them, they can smell an enemy a mile or two away. They also have a special friend in the egret, or tickbird, which is often seen riding on elephants' backs. This bird eats ticks and other insects that bother elephants. Tickbirds also cry out a loud warning to the elephants when danger is near.

Elephants that are not killed by man, other animals, or disease all die for the same reason. They starve to death. This happens because of the elephant's unusual teeth. In its lifetime, an elephant grows six sets of cheek teeth, the four huge teeth used to chew and grind food. As each set wears down, a new set grows in to take its place. The last set grows in when the elephant is around sixty years old. When this set wears down, it is not replaced. Unable to eat, the elephant dies.

OPOSSUMS

LIE: The opossum sleeps hanging upside down by its tail.

TRUTH: The opossum sleeps lying down.

No opossum can sleep hanging by its tail. The tail would relax and unwind. The opossum's tail is *prehensile*, which means it can be used like a fifth hand to grasp items. Although babies are able to hang from their tails, adult opossums are too heavy and would fall. Opossums sleep lying down in earthen dens, under porches, and in other safe havens.

The opossum is the only *marsupial* native to North America. A marsupial is an animal with a pouch for carrying its babies. Around eleven opossum babies are born at a time. They are hairless and blind, and each one is as small as your little fingernail. After they are born, they crawl through their mother's soft fur into her pouch, where they drink milk and keep warm while they finish growing. This cross-eyed, bald-tailed mammal grows to the size of a large cat and looks a lot like a giant rat.

Although the opossum is a slow runner with poor eyesight, it has managed to survive since the time of the dinosaurs. One of its best tricks is "playing 'possum." When danger approaches, the opossum falls down and plays dead. An attacker can poke it, bite it, and bark at it, but the opossum lies limp and won't move. Only when it is certain the danger is gone will the opossum continue on its way.

Opossums are not picky eaters. They are omnivores and don't care if their food is fresh and alive or dead and decaying. In the country, opossums may eat frogs, fruit, field mice, snakes, and vegetables. City opossums are often seen waddling down dark alleys, where they will do their late-night dining from garbage cans.

Virginia opossum (American 'possum)

OSTRICHES

LIE: The ostrich hides by burying its head in the ground.

TRUTH: The ostrich does not bury its head.

It's hard to tell how this old lie began. Very likely it started because this large African bird is almost always eating, bending over with its head close to the sandy ground looking for fruit, grass, insects, mice, and other goodies. From a distance an ostrich might look as if it were sticking its head into the sand.

An ostrich can't fly. It is the world's largest living bird, and its wings are too weak to lift its heavy body off the ground. A male ostrich might weigh three hundred and fifty pounds and grow to be seven and a half feet tall.

Since it can't fly away, the ostrich uses other ways to defend itself. Its best defense is running away. The ostrich is a fast runner—as fast as a horse. Its two powerful legs can pump along at about thirty-five miles an hour. If danger threatens when an ostrich is sitting on an egg, it will try to hide by flattening its body against the ground. An ostrich fights only when it can't run or hide. And what a fighter the ostrich is! It leaps high into the air, kicking out with its strong legs and knocking the enemy with the rock-hard claws on its two-toed feet.

Like all birds, the ostrich has no teeth and must swallow small, hard objects like stones and twigs to help it digest foods. These bits and pieces get stuck in the gizzard with the food the bird swallows. There the food and hard objects churn around together until the food has been ground up enough to be digested. Many a pet bird has died because no one put a little gravel in the bottom of its cage.

Rhea, an ostrich from South America

PORCUPINES

LIE: The porcupine can shoot its quills.

TRUTH: The porcupine cannot shoot its quills any more than you can shoot your hair.

For many years people thought porcupines could stand still and shoot quills out of their skin like bullets out of a gun. What else could explain the quills found stuck in the bark of a tree or in some poor dog's nose? We now know the only time quills "fly" is when the porcupine swishes its tail and a few quills drop out.

Each porcupine quill grows out of a hair follicle, the same way hairs grow on your body. As a quill matures, it becomes loosely attached. When a porcupine thinks it is in danger, its first defense is to run away. If it can't escape, the porcupine tightens its skin to make its thousands of quills stand on end, ready to stick into anything that touches them. Sometimes the porcupine will use an active defense, swishing its tail back and forth while backing towards its attacker. The loose quills come out easily, sticking into the nose and face of the would-be enemy. Just because a porcupine can't *shoot* quills doesn't mean it won't try to *stab* a few.

A porcupine has more than thirty thousand quills. Each quill is hollow, two to three inches long, sharp as a needle, and covered with scales. When a quill sticks into a warm animal, the animal's body heat makes the air inside the quill expand. This makes the nearly one thousand scales open like barbs to hold the quill firmly in place. The reason the mother porcupine is not hurt by her baby's quills when giving birth is that the baby's quills are soft. They become hard soon after birth.

Porcupines are mammals and belong to the rodent family. They are nocturnal, sleeping during the day and

North American porcupine

hunting food at night. A herbivore, the porcupine eats foods such as leaves, bark, berries, fruit, flowers, and grass. As people have moved into its territory, the porcupine has become fond of crops such as apples, corn, and cherries. Bananas are the top choice of porcupines living in captivity. And all porcupines like lots of salt in their diet.

Porcupines are good climbers. Their long, curved claws grip tree bark tightly. When bad weather threatens, many porcupines head for an apple tree, where they will be sheltered by the leaves and have a handy supply of a favorite food. If they sense a severe storm coming, porcupines will seek the thicker branches and denser leaves of an oak tree. The oak is a tall tree, and the more severe the storm, the higher porcupines seem to want to be. Porcupines are not fond of swimming but when they are forced into the water, the hollow quills act like a life jacket, helping them stay afloat until they can dog-paddle to safety.

Most animals know better than to tangle with a porcupine's sharp armor. For a long time, the porcupine's most dangerous natural enemy was the fisher. This giant weasel slipped its nose under the porcupine's quill-free belly, then quickly flipped it onto its back. The porcupine's soft belly was no defense against the fisher's sharp teeth and claws.

As the fisher grew scarce in the wild, either killed off by people or forced to search for safe shelter farther north, porcupines began having a population explosion. Today there are so many porcupines that they are no longer able to find enough food and salt in the woods. They have spread out and become a nuisance in towns and cities, eating people's gardens and chewing the bark off trees, which then die. Unlike the fisher, porcupines have learned to coexist with humans. In their quest for salt, porcupines chew on car tires and brake lines, which are coated with salt from winter roads. They'll also chew tool handles, tractor steering wheels, and anything else they can find that tastes of salt from human hands. Porcupines chew on these for salt the way we chew on gum for sugar, taking out the flavor and leaving the rest behind.

Porcupines would not be such a terrible problem if the fisher were still around. Fishers used to eat just enough porcupines to maintain the balance of nature. The remaining porcupines found all the food and salt they needed in the woods without having to destroy their surroundings. Some conservationists are now trying to bring back the fisher so people and porcupines can once again live together peacefully.

SNAKES

LIE: Snakes are wet and slimy.

TRUTH: The snake's skin is dry.

Snakes look wet and slimy because of the way light shines off their skin. What we call a snake's "scales" are really pieces of folded skin. These scales are very different from fish scales, which are separately attached to the skin and can be pulled out one at a time. The snake's overlapping skin makes a strong armor against enemies and rocky ground. Surrounding each scale is thinner connecting skin, like the skin between your fingers, that stretches as the snake moves.

Unlike mammals, which are always losing bits and pieces of old skin (that's the stuff you peel off after a sunburn or see floating on the bath water), snakes change skin all at once. Molting begins when a snake outgrows its old skin. If a snake eats enough, it can molt twelve or more times a year.

When molting begins, a snake's once-shiny skin grows dull. For a few days, the snake becomes quiet. It doesn't see well, doesn't feel well, and doesn't like being disturbed. When the snake is ready, it rubs its head against a tree or rock to loosen the old top layer of skin. Then, sliding forward, it peels out of the old skin like a foot out of a sock. The old skin usually slips off in one inside-out piece. In its place is shiny new skin that glitters and gleams in the light.

Some people believe a snake can sting with its tail or tongue. This isn't true. There is nothing in the tail or tongue that can hurt you. One of the most interesting snake tails belongs to the rattlesnake. The rattle sound is made when the snake shakes its tail, causing the rattles—rows of hardened skin on the end of the tail—to bump together. But the rattles cannot harm you. In fact, if you're lucky, the sound they make will warn you when a rattler's nearby.

A snake's tongue is no more dangerous than its tail. It looks dangerous because of the way the snake flicks it in and out of its mouth. But the Y-shaped tongue is soft and harmless. The reason the snake flicks its tongue is to find out what's going on. Is it hot outside? Is an enemy lurking? Is there a juicy mouse nearby? The flicking tongue picks up particles in the air and brings them inside the mouth. There, the two tips of the tongue slip into two holes in the roof of the snake's mouth. The holes are the *Jacobson's organ*, a sensitive taste organ. The snake "tastes" air with its tongue in much the same way you taste cake batter licked from your finger. Even blindfolded, you can taste the difference between chocolate and strawberry. So, too, can the snake "taste" enemy from prey.

There are some snakes whose bite can be dangerous to humans. This is because their *venom*—the chemicals they use to digest their food—is poisonous to people. Venom is injected by special teeth called *fangs*. Fangs can be hollow or grooved, curved or straight. When a poisonous snake bites to kill prey or defend itself, its venom flows through the fangs into the wound. Among the world's most poisonous snakes are the tiger snake, king cobra, common krait, and taipan. The four venomous snakes living in the United States are the copperhead, moccasin, rattlesnake, and coral snake. The coral snake is a member of the cobra family. The other three are pit vipers. Between their nostrils and eyes, pit vipers have small pits that sense heat. Going down into dark gopher holes, pit vipers can sense the warmth of a small animal up to twelve feet away.

Snakes have two eating problems. First, they have no hands to help them catch and hold their prey. Second, they have no chewing teeth to break their food into small pieces. Luckily, the teeth they do have are slanted backwards like barbs on a fishhook. When a snake strikes, it's hard for the prey to pull away.

30

Since the snake can't chew its meal, it must swallow everything whole. Unlike your jaws, which are firmly connected, the snake's jaws can swing far apart and move separately. After catching an animal, the snake begins pulling its prey in head first with its top teeth while holding on with the bottom teeth. Then it pulls the animal in with the bottom row of teeth while holding on with the top row. The snake's skin stretches to make room for its meal.

Once the prey is inside, the snake's digestive juices go to work. It takes several days to break down unchewed fur, bones, hair, skin, and feathers. Snakes don't need to eat often. Even when there is plenty of food around, they prefer to eat about once a month, digest the food, eliminate the waste, shed their skin, and start all over again. There are stories of snakes that have gone a whole year without eating. If a snake did survive such a long fast, it probably would be seriously ill from malnutrition or diseases caught in its weakened condition.

Snakes give birth in one of two ways. About half are *oviparous.* This means they lay tough, leathery-shelled eggs outside their bodies. Oviparous snakes must live where there is enough warm air, sun, and earth to incubate their eggs. Except for the python, snakes don't seem interested in hanging around to give their eggs the warmth they need to hatch. Not only does the python tend her eggs, she is also the only animal in the whole world able to raise her body temperature to incubate them.

The other snakes are *ovoviviparous.* They mostly live in cooler parts of the world and keep soft-shelled eggs inside their bodies until the babies are born. The babies emerge alive from the mother or are born inside a thin sac from which they quickly escape. Garter snakes are born this way. Once born, baby snakes are on their own. Even the mother python, who takes the time to make a nest and warm her eggs, ignores the babies once they hatch. But that's all right. Baby snakes can take care of themselves. They are born able to crawl, climb, swim, catch food, and eat.

Snakes never blink. They have no eyelids. What they do have is a transparent covering, like a built-in contact lens, that protects the eye from harm. That lens is part of the snake's skin and comes off when the snake molts. Just because their eyes are always open doesn't mean snakes are always seeing. When they sleep, their brains shut off their eyesight.

Snakes move quickly for animals with no legs. The fastest-moving snakes are the coachwhip and blue racer, both of which can travel four miles per hour. This is about the speed you go when you walk fast. If a snake can't run from danger, it may defend itself by hissing, hiding, playing dead, pretending it's going to strike, flattening itself to look bigger, or by trying to blend in with the background.

All snakes are carnivores. No snake eats plants. A few species of snakes eat insects, two eat frogs, one eats eggs, and one eats toads. All the rest prefer to eat furred or feathered herbivores.

Many people fear snakes, yet most snakes are harmless. The fact is, more people are killed in the United States each year by lightning than by snakebite. Even poisonous snakes don't like to fight. They strike in defense only when they feel cornered, startled, or frightened.

Snakes are interesting critters. People like looking at them and talking about them, which is how many myths, bits of misinformation, and lies have been spread. Some others are:

LIE: *Rattlesnakes will not cross a horsehair rope. Campers can sleep safely with such a rope in a circle around their sleeping bags.*

TRUTH: Although rattlers tend to shy away from things smelling of humans, they will crawl over a horsehair rope, or any other rope, in their way.

LIE: *You can tell a rattler's age by counting its rattles.*

TRUTH: A rattlesnake adds a rattle after each molting—up to twelve a year—and many of the old rattles scrape off on rocks.

LIE: *When you kill a snake, it will wait until sundown to die.*

TRUTH: Muscle reflexes can make a snake move for just a few minutes after it's dead.

LIE: *Frightened baby snakes will run inside their mother's mouth to hide when there's danger.*

TRUTH: Mother snakes pay little attention to their young. Besides, the babies wouldn't be able to breathe inside the mother.

LIE: *The hoop snake chases people by taking its tail in its mouth and rolling like a hoop.*

TRUTH: The hoop snake got its name because it lies in a hooplike circle. When it moves, it crawls along like other snakes. And it certainly doesn't go around chasing people!

LIE: *Some snakes fly.*

TRUTH: "Flying snakes" don't fly; they fall. These tree snakes jump from branches, flattening their bodies so they sort of plop to earth.

SPIDERS

LIE: The bite of a tarantula will kill you.

TRUTH: No tarantula is known to be dangerous to humans.

Years ago, the tarantula's bite was believed to be deadly. That was before scientists began to study this huge spider. So far, none of the many species discovered and studied has proven to be dangerous. What we call a spider's "poison" is really its *catabolic enzyme*, the same sort of digestive fluid our bodies use to digest food. Like that of most spiders, the tarantula's digestive fluid can kill insects but will leave nothing more serious than an itchy swelling on a human, if that.

It is not possible for a tarantula to walk up and bite you. Like other spiders, it has no teeth. A spider's so-called bite is really a pinch made with its two clawlike legs. The claws poke a couple of holes into which the spider drips some of that catabolic enzyme. A tarantula's claws are rarely used in defense but, even when they are, the tiny pinch is not painful to humans. The real purpose of the claws is to help the tarantula catch, hold, and shovel bugs into its mouth.

Why are people so afraid of tarantulas? Most likely it's because they are so big and hairy. The average tarantula is about five inches from leg tip to leg tip. One species of tarantula, the bird-eating spider, usually measures eight to ten inches and sometimes grows as large as fourteen inches—longer than the ruler you use in school! Many a filmmaker has scared audiences by showing a huge tarantula crawling up an actor's leg or arm. Luckily for the actor, the tarantula is harmless.

We tend to think of all creepy-crawlies as insects but tarantulas, like all spiders, are *arachnids.*

Some basic differences between arachnids and insects are:

• Spiders have eight walking legs. Insects have six.
• Insects have antennae. Spiders do not.
• The body of a spider is divided into two parts. An insect's body is divided into three parts.

Scientists have identified some fifty thousand different species of spiders. This may sound like a lot, but new species are found every year. Experts suspect there are many thousands of species yet to be discovered.

The tarantula eats its prey's body fluids and leaves the rest. A spider that eats its entire prey needs a little extra help. Before eating, the spider waits until its catabolic enzyme has softened the prey's tissues. By the time the spider begins to eat, most of its food has already been digested.

Although the tarantula is harmless to man, there are two North American spiders whose catabolic enzymes could possibly kill a human. These spiders, the black widow and the brown recluse, are most common in the South and West but can be found throughout the United States. Although they don't go out looking for people to attack, they will "bite" in self-defense. These spiders seek cool, dark places, like woodpiles, where they are sometimes startled by a person reaching in a hand to gather wood. Thinking it is being attacked, the spider defends itself. These bites are rarely fatal. Black widows and brown recluses help us by eating some of our most pesky insects like pill bugs and roaches.

One of the spider's best tricks is making silk inside its body. This silk is liquid until it comes out and hardens in the air. Spiders use their silk in many ways. Some tarantulas use their silk to line their underground nests. The strong silk also makes a fine "rope" to wind around food, tying it down until the spider is hungry.

Other spiders weave the fine strands of silk into beautiful webs that catch and hold insects. (The best time to see different web patterns is early morning, when hundreds of glistening dewdrops cling to the nearly invisible strands.)

Although the silk hardens after leaving the spider's body, it is not stiff and brittle like uncooked spaghetti. If it were, the web would shatter when insects flew into it. Instead, the silk stretches as much as twenty percent, forming a sticky net to trap and hold prey.

Spider silk is so flexible and strong that people once tried to make clothing from it. The silk was fine, every bit as beautiful as the silk we get from silkworms. Still, the experiment failed. Why? The thousands of spiders that were collected to produce the silk kept eating each other!

SQUIRRELS

LIE: A squirrel's bite will give you rabies.

TRUTH: A squirrel's bite can be very painful, but it is almost impossible for it to give you rabies.

If you ask your friends and family whether squirrels can give them rabies, it's likely many of them will say yes. For some reason, this lie is widely believed by a great many people. But the virus which causes rabies can begin only in meat-eating animals. For a herbivore like a squirrel to have rabies, it would have to be bitten by a rabid carnivore, and it would have to survive the attack. This would be an extremely unlikely event for two reasons. First, a rabid carnivore would be too sick to catch a healthy squirrel. And second, herbivores rarely survive attacks by carnivores.

There is a group of people in the United States who keep careful records of animal behavior all over the country. They work at the United States Center for Disease Control in Atlanta, Georgia. Counties in all the states collect information about animal diseases, habits, and attacks and send the information to Atlanta. The Center recently published a collection of reports on squirrels and other rodents from 1971 to 1983. The 1972 report said, in part, "There has never been a case of human rabies in this country attributed to rodent exposure, even though . . . an estimated twenty-four thousand rodent bites per year are severe enough to require medical consultation."

The strangest thing about squirrels is their front teeth—two incisors on top, two on the bottom—which *never* stop growing. The front surface of a squirrel's front teeth is harder than the back. This makes the teeth wear down at a sharp, chisel-like angle. All rodents have the same sort of front teeth. It is this slant that makes it possible for beavers to chew through trees, rats through walls, and tiny mice through cardboard boxes in the pantry. It is also why a rodent's bite can be so deep and painful.

Albino grey squirrel

Squirrels constantly chew and gnaw hard nuts and seeds that wear down their teeth. If a tooth becomes crooked, the squirrel is in terrible trouble. Instead of wearing down, the tooth keeps growing and becomes too long. It may poke up through the palate and into the brain, or it may even grow at an angle outside the mouth. Then the squirrel is unable to chew, and it starves to death.

The squirrel's tail is used in many ways. It bobs back and forth, helping the squirrel balance on tiny branches and run along thin telephone wires. When a squirrel leaps from one tree to another, its tail becomes a rudder to balance the body in flight. It can be held like an umbrella over the squirrel's head to ward off rain or create cooling shade. In winter, snuggled in its cozy nest, the squirrel wraps its tail around itself like a warm blanket.

You may have heard of flying squirrels. These squirrels don't really fly. They have a fold of extra skin attached to their front and back legs that looks like a furry cape or parachute. After climbing high up a tree, they can jump out, spread all four legs wide, and glide to the ground, the next tree, or wherever it is they want to go.

The squirrels we see most often are tree squirrels. They love to play, chasing each other up and around trees, over fences, and across roofs. They can race at amazing speeds because of the sure grip of their sharp clawed feet and their wonderful balancing tails. Sometimes tree squirrels make nests in hollow branches and tree trunks. More often their huge nests are built securely in the highest branches of sturdy old trees. These nests are tight weavings of leaves and twigs and bits of found twine and cloth. The tree squirrel's nest is hidden in summer when trees are covered with leaves. But in winter, when the large nests sit exposed on bare branches, we see how very many tree squirrels live all around us.

People believe squirrels hibernate because they are not seen often during cold winter months in the northern states. And in fact the squirrels do try to spend most of the bitter cold days snuggled in their nests. But they cannot go long without eating and must forage for food every few days. The only rodent that is a true hibernator is the groundhog. It does not eat or eliminate body waste from autumn until spring. In its deep sleep, its heartbeat falls from 150 beats a minute to 7 or 10, its body temperature drops from one hundred to thirty-seven degrees Fahrenheit, and it barely breathes at all. All its body functions slow to a deathlike state. Even the growth of its teeth becomes barely measurable.

Squirrels living where winters are cold begin growing a thick coat of fur in fall. They busily collect nuts and seeds to bury in the ground near their nests. It doesn't matter that the squirrels won't remember where they buried their food. Thanks to their keen sense of smell, they will be able to find other food, much of which was buried by other squirrels. Some of the seeds and nuts are never found. In spring, many take root and sprout, growing into new plants and trees that will provide food and homes for other squirrels in years to come.

MORE LIES PEOPLE BELIEVE

LIE: Birds hardly eat—thus, the expression "to eat like a bird."

TRUTH: Because of an enormously high metabolic rate (they burn up energy quickly), birds must eat most of the time they are awake. Some birds eat twice their body weight each day.

LIE: The chameleon hides from enemies by changing color to blend in with its background.

TRUTH: The chameleon does not decide when to change its color. Its color changes, usually from shades of brown to green or green to brown, when it becomes excited or when there is a change in light or temperature. By the way, what we know as chameleons are really American lizards called *anoles*.

LIE: You will die if you're bitten by a Gila monster or Mexican beaded lizard.

TRUTH: The Gila monster and the Mexican beaded lizard are the only poisonous lizards in the world. But even so, the bite of either is rarely fatal to humans.

LIE: Cheese is the best bait with which to catch mice and rats.

TRUTH: It's been found that mice in captivity don't even like cheese. Much better baits are peanut butter, vegetables, meat, and fresh fruit.

LIE: Bulls hate red.

TRUTH: Bulls, like most animals, are color-blind. When a bull is angry, it will attack whatever grabs its attention. In a bullring, this is the swirling red cape the matador waves at the bull.

Banded owl

LIE: Owls are wise.

TRUTH: Owls are not any wiser than other birds. This lie can be traced to ancient Greece where the owl was picked as the symbol for Athena, the goddess of wisdom. The owl is probably considered wise because it *looks* wise. Its large, dark eyes seem thoughtful and are surrounded by feathers that look like glasses.

Through the centuries, books and poems have reinforced the idea of the wisdom of owls. In "The Owl and the Nightingale," a thirteenth-century poem, the nightingale is bright and cheery while the owl is serious and thoughtful. More recently, cartoonists such as Disney have used the owl as a professor-type character.

LIE: If you touch a frog or toad, you'll get warts.

TRUTH: Neither animal can give you warts. The urine of a frog or toad can sting a cut, but this is harmless.

LIE: Camels store water in their humps and stomachs.

TRUTH: The camel's stomach is not nearly large enough to hold the twelve or more gallons of water a camel can drink at one time. Excess water is stored in tissues beneath the skin, to be used as the camel's body needs it. The camel's humps hold no water at all. Humps are mounds of fatty tissue that provide energy for the camel when it doesn't have enough to eat. As the fats in the humps are used up, the humps deflate like balloons with the air let out and flop to the side. After the camel eats, the humps again become firm.

LIE: Camels can travel for weeks on the desert without water.

TRUTH: To stay healthy, camels working in the hot desert should drink at least every three days and every day when possible. They can go longer, but their health would suffer. Camels are able to survive heat that would kill other animals. Their body temperature rises during the hottest part of the day so they absorb less heat. And a camel sweats very little, keeping fluids inside to nourish its body.

LIE: The whale, dolphin, and porpoise are fish.

TRUTH: They are mammals. They live in the water with fish but are warm-blooded, air-breathing, have fur (even if it's just a few stray hairs), and nurse their young through mammary glands.

LIE: Each year on February 2 the groundhog comes out of hibernation. If it sees its shadow, it knows there will be six more weeks of cold weather and it goes back to sleep. If the day is cloudy and the groundhog can't see its shadow, it knows there will be an early spring and it stays awake.

TRUTH: Groundhogs end their hibernations different times each year, usually much later than February 2. When they awaken from their long winter sleep, they are interested in eating and mating, not in the weather conditions. (And whether the day is cloudy or clear has no bearing on how long winter lasts.) The groundhogs we see in newspaper and television reports are awakened early for the occasion.

Eastern box turtle

LIE: The hippopotamus sweats blood.

TRUTH: The hippopotamus protects its tender skin from the hot sun by secreting a reddish oil that looks very much like blood.

LIE: All fish die if kept out of water too long.

TRUTH: The African lungfish digs into the mud at the start of the dry season and builds a kind of cocoon around itself before the sun-baked ground hardens. It sleeps, living on its own fat, for a year or more until water returns to the river.

LIE: A pack rat never takes something without leaving another item in its place.

TRUTH: A pack rat may drop an item it's carrying in order to pick up something new. Just as often, however, it will scamper off with some nice shiny object—a button, coin, or nail—without leaving another item in its place.

LIE: All turtles have hard shells.

TRUTH: There are soft-shelled turtles whose round, flat bodies are covered with flexible, tough skin. The leatherback sea turtle also has a soft covering.

LIE: You can tell a turtle's age by counting the rings on its back.

TRUTH: Some turtle shells have no growth rings at all. Also, a turtle in the warm South may grow at a faster rate than a turtle in the cold North and so will grow more rings on its shell over the same period.

BIBLIOGRAPHY

Burton, Maurice. *Animal Legends*. New York: Coward-McCann, 1956.

Crandall, Lee S. *A Zoo Man's Notebook*. Chicago: University of Chicago Press, 1966.

Dallinger, Jane. *Spiders*. Minneapolis: Lerner, 1981.

Fichter, George S. *Poisonous Snakes*. New York: Franklin Watts, 1982.

Hay, Keith G. *The Beaver's Way*. Washington, D.C.: National Wildlife Federation, 1973.

Hopf, Alice. *Biography of an Ostrich*. New York: Putnam's, 1974.

Lane, Margaret. *The Squirrel*. New York: Dial Press, 1981.

Rue, Leonard Lee III. *Meet the Opossum*. New York: Dodd, Mead, 1983.

Schlein, Miriam. *Billions of Bats*. New York: Lippincott, 1982.

———— . *Lucky Porcupine*. New York: Four Winds Press, 1980.

Scott, Jack. *Alligator*. New York: Putnam's, 1984.

Shuttlesworth, Dorothy. *The Story of Rodents*. New York: Doubleday, 1971.

Stewart, John. *Elephant School*. New York: Pantheon, 1982.

Stonehouse, Bernard. *A Closer Look at Reptiles*. New York: Gloucester Press, 1979.

Winkler, William G. "Rodent Rabies in the United States." *The Journal of Infectious Diseases*, Volume 126, Number 5. Atlanta: The Center for Disease Control, 1972.

Zim, Herbert S. *Ostriches*. New York: Morrow, 1958.

INDEX

SUSAN SUSSMAN's office is in Evanston, Illinois, in the Noyes Cultural Arts Center, an old school building converted into artists' studios. It was in the Noyes gym that she first met Robert James and his wonderful traveling zoo. The lie/truth he told about squirrels and rabies sparked the idea for this book. *Lies (People Believe) about Animals* is Sussman's eighth book for young people. Other books published by Albert Whitman are *Hippo Thunder; There's No Such Thing as a Chanukah Bush, Sandy Goldstein;* and *Casey the Nomad*. Sue Sussman lives in Evanston with her husband, Barry, and their three children, Aaron, Rachael, and Sy.

ROBERT JAMES's office is in many places—a zoo compound in southern Illinois; a fully equipped traveling zoo housed in a huge brown truck; and, occasionally, the gym in Evanston, Illinois, where he first met Sue Sussman. For the past seventeen years, James and his zoo have traveled from Canada to Mexico to present his program "Animal Encounters, Inc." He currently visits about four hundred schools a year, providing young audiences with hands-on experiences that help teach the truth about wild animals.

James received his doctorate in zoology from San Diego State University, has directed zoos across the country, and written many scientific articles and books. He spends his summers in research. This is his first book for young people.

FRED LEAVITT has heard many lies about photographers in his twenty years of freelancing. One is that a photographer needs a large studio and lots of expensive equipment in order to photograph an elephant. The truth is that all of the animals represented in this book were photographed against white seamless paper with a hand-held, 35mm Nikon camera and portable lights. The only anxious moment the photographer experienced was when he was left alone in a small room with a large alligator that decided to crawl off the white paper.

Leavitt's previous books include *Pullman: Portrait of a Landmark Community* and *Fred Leavitt's Chicago*. He lives on the north side of Chicago with his wife, Margit, and son, Adam—who assisted his father with the photographing of these animals but wasn't anywhere around when the alligator crawled off the paper.